Prepping with Moderation

Preparing For the Worst While Living for the Best: Volume 1

by
Steve Chianos

Table of Content

Introduction

When most people hear the word "prepper," they instantly think of a stereotype that has been propagated by TV and other media for a long time. Chances are when you hear that word, you also think of a person living on the edge of the world, hoarding things that they don't really need. Let's take a moment to correct that image.

Preppers are people who live on the fringes of society, burying shipping containers to create a bunker and living off the water they pump from a nearby stream, right? They keep chickens and goats, try to grow their own produce, and have 2 years' worth of MREs stored in that bunker, right?

Well, not exactly. This is what much of the mainstream media wants you to believe. To be fair, some of these stereotypes are rooted in a few truths. There are people out there building bunkers and setting up solar stills to purify water. There are indeed people out there planning for a complete societal collapse, ready to deal with the economy failing, proudly self-sufficient.

However, the reality of prepping is different from the hype. As a matter of fact, there's a fair chance that you are probably already a prepper on some level.

If you make sure you have a generator and some fuel on hand in case there's a blackout, you're a prepper because you are ready to deal with any potential power outage. If you have a family fire drill, you're prepared for a disaster that you pray would never come. Who wouldn't want to keep their refrigerators running and water flowing in case of an emergency?

That's "Prepping with Moderation!" You're not preparing for a complete societal collapse. You're not preparing to be fully self-sufficient for years and ultimately rebuild society. You're preparing to survive a short-term event with as little disruption to your life as possible. Prepping with Moderation is preparing for an event that you hope will never happen. Unfortunately, sometimes they do happen.

Until recently, those events were few and far between, and their effects in most of those cases were on such a small scale that most of us have never needed to think about preparing for these emergencies. However, COVID 19 turned all our lives upside down. Shortages of basic supplies that were common in poorer countries were no longer exclusive to those places. It was a worldwide phenomenon that affected anyone and everyone.

Poor utility planning didn't take into account years of climate disasters, and the Texas power grid froze as a result. Literally froze. Hundreds of thousands of people were without power in freezing weather with no means to heat their homes or provide themselves with water. Without heat, buildings and houses froze, and millions of dollars worth of property damage were the outcome.

As we were finally starting to come out of the pandemic, hackers shut down the Colonial pipeline, which supplied 45% of the fuel to the eastern US. Suddenly, people who were just starting to get their businesses opened back up found themselves unable to find fuel to get to work. The prices of fuel spiked, and the cost of goods in the stores rose accordingly.

None of these events were society-ending, but they were life-altering and should have shown us that we should all be doing a little bit of prepping. We should all be figuring out what is a rational amount of life essentials to keep on hand just in case. How many cases of Costco TP do we need? How should you rotate cases of water to keep them fresh? Canned tuna or dry pasta? These are details that might not have crossed your mind a few years ago, but they should now. The pandemic and these global events showed us that we are vulnerable, and our lives can be turned upside down in just one day.

And that's why you're not crazy for thinking about doing your own prepping!

Section 1: Rational Reasons You Should Start Prepping

Chapter 1: Environmental Caused Shortages

Before we can delve into your preparations for extreme situations and life-changing global events, you need to understand the potential risks that you might encounter. Nature can be ruthless at times, and in its ruthlessness, we stand to suffer much. These natural disasters that we are about to discuss are not some distant possibilities. They happen more often than you'd think, which is why you need to prep yourself and be self-sufficient for some time until life returns to some normalcy.

Hurricanes and Tropical Storms

Unfortunately, hurricanes are some of the most occurring natural disasters that spare nothing and no one in their paths. The United States, in particular, has always had a rough time dealing with them, which allowed some hurricanes to wreak havoc and cause billions in property damage, not to mention take hundreds of lives. In 2005, Hurricane Katrina caused close to 2,000 deaths and left several US states in ruins, causing over $125 billion in damage. The problem with hurricanes is they cause severe damage within a 50-150 miles radius, destroying much in their paths. A traditional hurricane can have a devastating effect on the environment and damage trees and could potentially have long-term ecological ramifications on the affected area.

Also known as typhoons, hurricanes are tropical cyclones that consist of an eye of the storm that is surrounded by a vortex of fast-moving wind and rainstorms. Wind speeds can reach hundreds of miles per hour, which can sweep anything in its path. In short, hurricanes occur when warm air from a thunderstorm over an ocean and the air at the surface of the ocean rise and create an area of low pressure. Cooler air is pulled downward toward the ocean, and the formed storm moves at great speed across the water.

Earthquakes

You already know what an earthquake feels like. It's when there's a sudden movement in the earth's plates (a jolt of sorts in the tectonic plates), which causes the ground to shake in varying degrees. This could last from a few seconds up to a few minutes. Sometimes, earthquakes start off mild, and the shaking grows violent quite fast. The problem with earthquakes is the fact that they happen suddenly and without warning, so they could have some devastating effects if the earthquake is severe. However, earthquakes happen every day around the world, and they don't always cause significant damage. The US alone was reported to have over 3,000 in 2015. Yet, even a minor earthquake can be a source of emotional distress and trouble for a lot of people.

However, some earthquakes can leave you without power or water for days or even weeks. If an earthquake is powerful enough, it can cause significant damage to the power grids, roads, and much more. It could even lay waste to an entire city. Some even leave the environment itself in serious danger and compromise wildlife and the flow of river and sea waters, among other serious disasters.

Tsunamis

One of the most deadly consequences of an earthquake is a tsunami. It could also be caused by volcanic eruptions or explosions under the ocean. Violent disturbances like these can cause the seabed to erupt and displace huge amounts of water, which could then sweep cities on the shore, killing thousands and destroying property. The large waves that result after a jolt like this to the seabed travel at great speed and cannot be stopped, especially if the waves come from deep water. Upon reaching the coast, their speed decreases, but unfortunately, their height increases, meaning they can be several feet high and impossible to escape. In 2004, an Indian Ocean earthquake caused tsunami waves that were 100 ft (30 m) high upon reaching inland! The tsunami killed almost 230,000 people and destroyed countless livelihoods, leaving many without food, water, shelter, or power.

Tornadoes

Also known as cyclones, tornadoes are a cyclone of air that moves swiftly as it comes in contact with earth's surface. A tornado is the result of humid air heating up and rising to meet cold air, which forms thunder clouds. This, combined with the winds coming from different directions, causes the air to spin, which leaves us with the familiar sight of the funnel in the air. Tornadoes can be short, or they could last for some time, and they often cause power outages and paralyze public services and lead people to panic-buy.

Floods

Floods are another common natural disaster that is quite frequent in countries like the US. In simple terms, a flood is when usually dry land gets flooded by water as a result of a tornado or tsunami, or in some cases, dam failures. Excessive rainfall can also cause floods. Floods can cause significant damage and destroy property, including houses and cars, and they also kill many people. Floods often leave states in a complete shutdown, and people don't have access to basic services and food/water supplies for quite some time until the situation is dealt with.

Droughts

Droughts are the exact opposite of floods. They happen when land that usually has plentiful water supplies whether from rainfall or other sources, experiences long periods of less water. This can kill crops and negatively impact agriculture. Droughts often lead to famine since many farmers don't have access to the food they usually would have if there was water. Like floods, it helps if you have some food stored to deal with a drought.

Blizzards

For those living in areas where winter storms are frequent, prepping is not a luxury or an option. Blizzards are often accompanied by fast winds and can completely shut down cities and towns for days because first, the snowstorm has to settle down, and then the authorities have to clear the snow from the roads so you could go get food, water and basic supplies.

Pandemics

As we've learned from COVID-19, pandemics can be some of the most serious global disasters that affect millions of lives. Like COVID, many scientists believe that most pandemics start with the transmission of an animal microbe to a human. Almost all the worst pandemics that humanity has experienced started with some animal. In some cases, the animals are the source of the infection, and in others, they are not the original source but rather a carrier. Examples across history include bovine tuberculosis, which is transmitted from cows to humans and caused several outbreaks in the 19th century. It could also be transmitted to other animals, not just humans. Then you have other examples like bird flu (Avian influenza), which caused serious outbreaks not too long ago. These pandemics can significantly affect our food supplies since animals are the main source of food for many people around the world. An outbreak like COVID-19 can also keep people at home and drive many to panic-buy, which is where prepping proves important.

Chapter 2: Man Caused Shortages

As fierce and ruthless as nature might sometimes be, man can often be much worse. The environment can, in many ways, be responsible for food, water, and power shortages, but it is not the culprit in all cases. Sometimes, we bring terrible shortages like these upon ourselves and our fellow man.

Conflict and Policy Changes

Since the dawn of time, human beings have entered into one conflict after the other, and most of the time, they are futile and pointless. Food supply chains have become international over the past few decades. Few countries, if any ever, are entirely self-sufficient when it comes to food supplies, which means that nations have become interdependent when it comes to the food supply. A country that has grain fields might not be able to produce enough rice or other essential produce. While this is a good thing, it can also be quite risky. If tensions arise between two countries that are reliant on each other's food supply chains, this can lead to serious conflict, and one might hold the other's basic need for a certain food hostage until the conflict is resolved. Countries often try to take protective measures to increase their food security, but there is only so much that they can do. The problem is, those affected the most by such conflicts are the citizens of those nations that might one day be faced with an unexpected shortage in bread, rice, or other essential food supplies that they cannot do without.

Policy changes can also have a negative impact on food supplies. Countries might impose higher import taxes on food supplies, which might lead to foreign exporters not doing business or stalling. One of the most significant problems a person might encounter is if their country raises prices on food supplies all of a sudden, which can have disastrous consequences. People hoard if they hear about an impending rise in food prices, and you might find yourself unable to find some essentials that you need all of a sudden.

Sabotage

Sometimes, the disruption and shortages to the basic needs of others are intentional and deliberately done as an act of pure evil. A most recent example of that is the Colonial Pipeline hacking which happened a few months ago. Hackers stole a compromised password that granted them access to the systems of the largest fuel pipeline in the United States. On May 7, 2021, a week after the culprits got a hold of the leaked password, the company received a ransom demand. As a precaution, Colonial Pipeline shut down the entire operation to avoid any further compromise to their data and network—a first in the system's almost 60-year-old history.

With 2.5 million barrels transported daily through the company systems, the entire gulf coast was quickly affected. Lines began piling up at gas stations, and prices were at their highest in years. Panic buying started, and people were in a frenzy to keep themselves secured during one of the most dangerous crises an area could face. Shortages happened in Florida, Georgia, Alabama, and other states, with Southern Carolina and Southern Virginia suffering significant shortages in most gas stations. The company ended up paying the ransom and made sure their system was secured to avoid any further attacks.

Another recent attack targeted JBS, the world's largest meat processing company. The cyber-attack compromised JBS operations in Canada, Australia, and the US. Using ransomware to encrypt the company data, a hacking group called REvil forced the company to pay $11 million as ransom. Attacks like these compromise food supplies in many places around the world, forcing people to panic buy, and in many cases, they don't even get the chance to buy meats and store them because they run out quite fast.

Contamination

Accidental or intentional contamination of produce can be another disastrous man-caused shortage that affects many lives. Negligence is one of the main reasons why this might happen. Contamination can happen before harvest or during the cleaning, handling, packaging, and transportation of the products. Foodborne pathogens have been on the rise in recent years, and in many cases, outbreaks happen with crops of fruit and vegetables, which can be disastrous on many levels. Affected products include eggs, dairy products, poultry and meat, and just about any fruit and vegetable you can think of. These pathogen outbreaks can cause a variety of diseases like salmonella and E. coli do.

So, why do they happen? A lot of different factors can contribute to contaminated produce. It begins at the watering phase. If farmers use water that is contaminated or unfit for crops, this could contaminate plants, and in turn, they carry pathogens into the crops that we end up consuming. Farmers who do this might be negligent on purpose because it saves time or money, and effort. Sometimes, it's the source's fault. Water treatment plants might not have properly treated sewage water (which is often used in irrigation), and if that happens, they risk a plethora of pathogens attaching themselves onto the plants and produce—the animals, too, since in many cases, cattle eat from the pasture grass that could be contaminated if the water is unclean. This means that the cow's milk and meat will be contaminated as well.

Whether it's because of policy change, foul work, or produce contamination, these are just examples of man-caused food shortages that can affect you in a blink of an eye. You could wake up one day and find that there is no available milk, vegetables, or meat for the above mentioned reasons, and if you're not prepared, your family will most likely suffer.

Chapter 3: Utility Failures

Whether it's caused by man or Mother Nature, utility failures are just as important to prepare for as food shortages. A power outage can last for days, if not more in some extreme cases, and if you don't have a contingency plan, it can be life-threatening. The same goes for gas and water shortages.

Power

The first utility failure that you have to prepare for is a power outage. As we mentioned earlier, blizzards, hurricanes, floods, and other natural disasters can affect everyday life in more ways than one. It's more than likely that in a thunderstorm or heavy rain, the power grid in your town could be compromised. In a storm, if you don't have power, how else will you keep the food in your fridge from spoiling, or how will you get anything done without light or electricity? To delve deeper into the subject, let's understand how and why a power outage can happen.

It doesn't always have to be extreme weather that causes an outage. Sometimes, a simple lightning strike at the wrong place can cause utility failures. Lightning is one of the most common reasons for power outages since it can hit electrical equipment and cause a surge that would bring the grid down. A lightning bolt hitting a tree can also cause it to fall over and take down power lines with it. In extreme cold, ice buildup on power lines can stop them from working. Ice can even freeze a tree limb and make it much heavier, and it can fall on power lines and cause an outage.

High winds might lead to the same outcomes. Not only can it be so powerful it would take down power lines, but it can also break tree limbs and even blow an entire tree off its roots and into a power line, causing a circuit failure. Floods are another natural disaster that can cause significant damage to aboveground and underground electrical equipment and shut them down for days.

Reading this, you might think that you're safe from power outages because you live in an area where you don't get many hurricanes and floods or even rain. Yet, there's something else that you have to keep in mind. Aging power grids are another leading reason for blackouts. Believe it or not, you can find some power lines in the US that date back to the late 1880s! Most of the electrical grid in the country today dates back to over 70 years ago, constructed in the 50s. While these grids were initially designed with a future increase in population accounted for, they are old now, and many of them are at capacity. This is why blackouts are becoming more and more frequent as the years go by. In 2015, there were over 3,500 outages reported in the US. The numbers keep getting worse by the year, too. Utility companies are often slow with the maintenance of power lines, which also reflects on the eventual performance. In times of cold snaps and heatwaves, power grids are especially under more stress, which leads to more frequent blackouts.

Water

Water shortages occur when the water main breaks, which causes leakage out of the pipe through the cracks and/or holes. In most cases, water still flows through the pipe, but the pressure is significantly less. The leaks also often damage the pipe, meaning the fix might be delayed, or bigger problems with water mains might arise in the future.

Water main breaks can happen for a host of different reasons, the most being age and heat/cold. The older the pipe, the more likely it will suffer from breaks due to wear and tear. On the other hand, temperature variations are just as dangerous. When the ground is cold, sometimes freezing, this applies additional pressure on the pipe that it simply wasn't designed to deal with. The water inside the pipe might sometimes even freeze, which greatly lowers the pressure inside the pipe. High temperatures, on the other hand, might cause the ground in which the pipes are placed to crack and shift, which creates tension in the pipes and leads to cracks.

Another problem that might cause water shortages is contamination. In some cases, poorly installed pipe fittings and systems might lead to contamination. Cross-connections to other water sources also increase the likelihood of contamination infecting the water in the pipes.

Gas

Like with water, there are several risks that could affect a natural gas line. Distributed through underground pipelines, natural gas disruptions are not as frequent as power outages, but they can be far more dangerous, and they are also much more complicated to fix. A break in a natural gas pipeline can lead to explosions and fires, and gas leaks are a health danger in general. Repairs can take weeks and possibly even months until the gas flow is restored to its normal operations.

Gas pipeline disruptions can happen because of extreme weather conditions like storms and flooding. Extreme cold can also severely affect pipelines, as happened with Texas in the recent cold wave that left thousands shivering in the cold without any means to keep themselves warm. Without getting into the technical details, suffice to say that Texas's natural gas infrastructure was not designed to deal with such cold temperatures, and it faltered during that winter storm.

Section 2: Getting Started

Chapter 4: How Much Is Too Much?

Prepping is about balance. As we've explained throughout the past few chapters, there are many disasters that could happen and leave you stranded in the face of hunger, thirst, and the cold. You cannot and should not rely on the National Guard or other emergency rescue agencies to come save you. There is no telling when they would come for you if they could at all. This is why prepping is important. Yet, you also shouldn't hoard years' worth of supplies. Chances are, much of it will go to waste, and you'll have just spent a lot of money and taken supplies that others might have needed. The key is in finding the right balance between being not prepared at all and preparing for the apocalypse.

How Much Food and Water Should You Store?

This is the first question that you need to ask yourself. First of all, are you just storing food for yourself, or do you have family members to take into consideration? You need to at least work out the caloric intake of you and your family members so that you can eat sufficient meals and keep yourself going until the emergency resolves. So, taking into account how much food you and your household need per day, how much food should you store?

To answer that question, you need to consider the location in which you live. How likely are certain disasters to happen where you live? Do you get constant blackouts because of fast winds or storms year-round? Do you live by the coast, so there are high chances of hurricanes? Have there been any incidents in the past where the water lines in your area have been contaminated? It's crucial that you ask these questions because, as we said, you don't want to store more food and water than you need. While it is impossible to predict what kind of weather events might happen, you should still take into account previous patterns and occurrences.

General guidelines by organizations advise that you have at least one week's worth of food and water stockpiled for each family member and pet—yes, you should take your pets' supplies into consideration. However, it is more than likely that the economic shutdown or emergency situation might last longer than that. If you live in a high-risk area in terms of natural disasters, experts recommend storing at least three months' worth of supplies for your households. In previous incidents like Hurricanes Sandy and Katrina, it took a long time for emergency responders to get to people. Moreover, it took months for the food supply to return to normal, which is why preppers were fortunate in such a terrible disaster because their needs were relatively covered during that time.

Some people stockpile food and supplies in extra as an act of good faith so they can help their neighbors in case the emergency lasts for longer than expected. Yes, there are still good people in the world. While you don't have to do that, if you can manage it, this would definitely be a great thing because you'll be able to help neighbors and other distressed families in times of crisis.

Power

Food and water aren't the only things that you will need to cover. In the two hurricanes mentioned above, some people had to make do with generators for almost two months until power grids were restored. While you don't need something as big as what's in a hospital or a factory, you should get yourself a generator that can keep your household going in the heat or cold, not to mention help you keep appliances like the TV and washing machines running. Candles are always a bad idea. They are a fire hazard, and to keep a house well-lit, you will need many, which further increases the risk of a fire. Always use battery or solar-powered lamps and flashlights. It's also recommended that you install battery-operated smoke and carbon monoxide detectors—running generators in the wrong way can cause high carbon monoxide emissions, which can be lethal.

Solar panels are another great idea that can keep you going for long in case of power outages. A system of solar panels can keep your refrigerator running and also any pumps you might be using around the house, which are essentials to keep you going during an emergency blackout. Take some time to research the generator options so you can get one that will help you for as long as possible. Bigger houses with a lot of appliances that need powering require generators with high power output. If you, on the other hand, don't care about how many appliances to run but rather want a generator that can last for long, look for ones with high continuous operating time. Pro tip: stock up on the generator's fuel. If you have a great generator with no way to fuel it, then it's as good as useless.

Chapter 5: Water Storage for the Short Term

In emergencies, water is the most important thing there is. You can go for days with little food, but without enough water, you might not survive. This is why you have to consider your water needs depending on possible disasters and how you should store the water.

In general, a person needs one gallon (about 3.7 liters) of water per day, and these are the numbers you should have in mind when you prepare for an emergency. As we mentioned earlier, you will store enough for each member of your household; the more, the better. People's hydration needs differ, but any person can get by on a gallon per day, which should be more than enough during catastrophes.

For short-term prepping, it is recommended that you keep a minimum of 1-2weeks' worth of water in case you are stranded and can't have access to clean drinking water. This is for small-scale emergencies like power outages or blizzards that would keep you from going to get water for a week or so. However, it would be wise if you store more than just your family's basic drinking needs. You will need more water for cooking, and you'll most likely need it for hygiene, so it's always best to take these factors into consideration.

Moreover, another reason to stock up on a bit more than your needs is in case the municipal water takes a few days to get back on track. It might be a good idea to keep drinking your clean, safely stored water for a few days until you are 100% certain that mains are functional and uncontaminated.

Storage Options

A key angle to remember about water storage is how you're going to do it. You can't exactly store your drinking water in the bathtub and hope it will remain clean. Storing drinking water in open containers is never a good idea, and it's something that you have to avoid at all costs. For short-term storage, your best option is jerry cans. Sure, there are larger barrels that you can use to store larger quantities, but jerry cans stand out because they are portable, and you can easily move them around even when they're full.

Jerry cans are also cheap and can carry up to 5 to 7 gallons, so you can store a person's weekly supply of water in just one jerry can. They also come in several materials, some of which are quite tough and can withstand accidental falls and even an earthquake. The last thing that you need is for your short-term water supply to be compromised.

Whatever storage options you use, you have to make sure that the water is available for consumption at all times. You need to have 1-2weeks' worth of water available and easily accessible because this is what it means to have emergency water prepped. For short-term emergencies, you shouldn't have to work on searching or filtering the water, and you certainly won't be able to make a store run for some. So, always have it ready, so you can consume this water if a disaster strikes and you find your normal supply compromised.

Chapter 6: Water Purification for the Mid Term

If you plan on prepping for water emergencies for a duration of over two weeks to a month, then you will have to take a few points into consideration. When it comes to hydration, the catch is in consuming good, uncontaminated water that wouldn't cause you any illness. This works by focusing on two details: how you're going to store the water for the mid-term and how you're going to purify it in case you have some doubts about the purity of the source. Remember that drinking water is as important as air if you're stranded, so you cannot risk drinking unclean water or else you'd jeopardize your family's wellbeing.

Storing Water for Over Two Weeks

Some materials work for storing water; others don't. You can use enamel-lined metal, plastic, and glass containers to use drinking water. What you should avoid are containers that have harmful materials or certain plastics that can react with the water if stored for three or four weeks. Moreover, never use containers that were used to hold toxic materials for water storage. It might sound like a no-brainer, but the idea of washing that bleach bottle and using it for storing water might be tempting, but it can also be lethal, so never do that.

Rotating stock containers for storing water is never a good idea. Unless it was used to store food, you don't want to use that container to store water for a few weeks. Some people consider recycling juice or milk cartons, for instance, but that isn't wise. You can properly wash them, but there's a good chance that they will still keep some of the bacteria that could be mixed with the water and cause health problems. Saving a few dollars on container options isn't really worth it.

The rotation system with bottled water is also pretty risky when it comes to water storage, so you have to play it safe. It might sound perfectly reasonable to buy bottled water and daily refill the bottles for emergencies. That way, you can replenish your water stock without having to invest in new containers. However, in reality, using bottled water containers for storage is a bad idea. For starters, they are single-use items meant to be used once and then disposed of. This makes them ill-prepared for mid-term storage of a few weeks.

Plastic water bottles are also very easy to crack, break, and wear down much faster than other containers. Do you really want to risk your emergency water supply on fifty or a hundred of these? Speaking of numbers, these bottles can only store so much water. It'd be extremely time- and space-consuming to store water in single-use bottles as opposed to containers that can house 5 or 7 gallons each. Not only that, but bottled water is also very hard to move in large quantities. Say you have your bottled water supply stored in a shed a few hundred feet from your house. If the weather is terrible out there, you'd have to make dozens of runs to the shed to get those bottles because you'll only be able to carry a few at a time. On the other hand, two larger containers can do the job of a dozen water bottles, so they're definitely easier to move in bulk.

Bottled water is also worse for the environment. It creates so much plastic waste that could just be done without. They're expensive, too. Why spend so much money on bottled water when you can use the tap?

To summarize, your best way for storing water over a period of 2-4 weeks is containers that can hold several gallons each. Stay away from plastic bottled water, and don't try to use the bathtub to store your drinking water. It's unclean, and it also doesn't have enough room. A family of four needs about 80 gallons of water for a period of three weeks. To store that much, you need to buy bigger containers and think practically.

Cleaning and Purification

Storing water for a mid- or even long-term crisis isn't just about finding the right containers or doing the math. It's also about making sure your water remains pure and clean. This starts before you even store the water. You can't just buy a container, fill it with water, and hope for the best. You need to properly store it so you can be certain it's safe for drinking when the time comes.

Expert opinions vary on whether or not you should purify the water before you store it. Assuming you'll be using tap water, it might not be a bad idea to purify the water before storage, especially if you have doubts about the quality of the municipal water supplies. If you want to purify the water and then store it, use chlorine bleach, which prevents the growth of microorganisms and can keep your water pure for extended periods of time. If you're going to get water from another source like a well or lake, then you should definitely use chlorine as a safety precaution. Just add a quarter of a teaspoon of the chlorine bleach per gallon of stored water, stir, and wait for half an hour before drinking it.

Tips for Safe Storage

Clean the Container: Before you add chlorine bleach or water, you have to make sure that the container is cleaned. Just fill it with some warm water and dish soap, shake the container, and rinse/drain. This will get any debris or dust out of the container. Then, add chlorine bleach and some water, and rinse/drain. Doing this ensures that the container itself is clean and safe for water storage.

Rotate the Water: Stored water might begin to change color, taste, and/or odor after a while, no matter how well it is stored. Factors like the initial quality of the water, temperature, and the container play into this. So, it's always best that you regularly rotate your supply to avoid having to use unclean water if an emergency happens. In theory, the stored water can last for a couple of years, but we don't recommend waiting for that long. Instead, rotate your supply every 3-4 months.

Get the Right Plastic: We mentioned earlier that you could use plastic containers for water storage, but that doesn't mean any plastic. Make sure you're using a plastic type that is suitable and approved for water storage. If you don't know how to make sure that the plastic is good, ask the store clerk to help you.

Store Properly: As we mentioned earlier, you want water to last for a few weeks in case of a mid-term emergency. For that to happen, you have to properly store it. Keep it stored away from light and heat (the sun basically) as well as any potential bacteria. So, wash your hands before you store water, and make sure the containers are tightly shut to avoid having any contaminants affecting your supply. Also, in the case of plastic containers, you should know that plastic can absorb certain chemicals, so you have to be careful where you put the containers. Stay away from cement floors and other locations that might put the plastic in contact with harmful chemicals that might affect the water quality.

Mind the Temperature: When you store water, you should take potential temperatures into consideration. Water expands when it freezes, so if you live in an area where it might be that cold, you shouldn't fill your containers to the brim because water will expand, and it might break the container if frozen.

Chapter 7: Water: How to Find It and Purify It over the Long Term

The main challenge of long-term crises, when it comes to water storage, is how unexpected they are. Even the best of preppers never know how long a crisis might affect the water supply. For short- and mid-term crises, anything under a month or so basically, you can make-do and will most likely find an answer to storing drinking water. If the problem persists for over a month, though, then you will have to get creative because it is more than likely that you won't have enough stored to last that long.

Finding a Water Source

Fortunately, there are some clever ways that you can find water in times of disaster that you weren't prepared for. Before we get to the not-so-well-known sources, let's talk about the obvious ones that you should consider first. To prep for a disaster, you need to think ahead. You shouldn't wing it and rely on your stored water containers because some disasters might last for longer than a month, which means your drinking water will quickly run out.

Natural We're talking about lakes, wells, rivers, and other natural sources that might prove quite useful in times of emergency. When it comes to those sources, you have to know about them before a hurricane or another crisis strikes. Don't wait for a disaster to pick up a map and figure out what nearby water sources are there. The last thing that you need in times of a crisis like a blizzard or a thunderstorm is to leave your house and wander aimlessly in search of a well or nearby lake.

So, one of the essential pillars of prepping is having potential nearby water sources marked on a map, from creeks and streams to lakes and rivers. You can use paper maps or GPS technology even.

Just figure out whether there are water sources around your place. It doesn't have to be a well or a large lake. Many of the smaller brooks and streams are hidden and can provide your family with much-needed drinking water.

When it comes to moving water from sources like these, you need to give yourself options. Water is heavy, and if you're not prepared, you might not make much use of the creek or river water. Your first option to transport water is water jugs, containers, and jerry cans like we mentioned earlier. Have a few spare ones available in your house so you can use them to move water from the natural source to your residence.

Another way to transport water is wagons and carts, which can be easily filled and moved to your home if the lake or river is nearby. You might be worried about the purity of water moved in a wagon or cart, but you will purify it before using it, so there's no problem there. The most important thing is transporting the water, and once that is done, you will be able to filter it.

Other Sources

What if you live in an area where there are no natural water sources, and you need emergency water because the disaster has affected the supply for too long? There are a few more options that you can consider if you haven't stored enough water for long-term crises. These are to be considered after trying wells, lakes, and other natural options.

The average water heater tank can store anything between 40 and 120 gallons of water, which can prove invaluable in emergencies. Before you can use this water, you need to turn off the electricity or gas supply so you can avoid any potential accidents since you'll be emptying that tank. Then, open the drain valve located at the

ter getting rid of the cloudiness that affected the water, you can
gin to purify it. Boiling is always the better option of the two,
ough it might not always be available. Boil the water you want to
rify for 10 to 15 minutes. Don't boil it for too long, though,
cause some of the water will evaporate, and this is an emergency,
 you need as much water as you can spare. Let the water cool
fore you drink it, but cover it as it does to avoid having it
ntaminated again. Or you can use the bleach technique we
entioned above to purify your water.

ne thing to keep in mind is the urgency to act quickly. If you hear
. the news that an emergency is happening, don't wait for the
itcome. If you're not prepared, you can still save the day and store
 lot of water in a short time. Fill the bathtub and any large
ntainers that you can find with water so you can store as much as
ou can before the supply is compromised. This is not the ideal way
 store water, but you'll be able to get around to doing it right and
urifying it when the water supply does get cut off.

bottom of your tank and drain that water into con
anything you have prepared for emergency storage.

The pipes and plumbing around your house also car
gallons of water that can be used in case of emergencies
not least, as a last-ditch effort, you can use the tank of yo
the tank, not the bowl since you won't most likely hav
resources to purify something as contaminated as the wa
bowl. With these hidden sources of water, purification
utmost importance because this water can and will most
contaminated, so you have to clean it first before dr
cooking.

Purification

As we just mentioned, treatment is a must if your
contaminated or if you have to get water from unorthodox
Contaminated water doesn't just taste or smell bad. It ca
very dangerous because the microorganisms in it ca
anything from cholera to typhoid and hepatitis, and
emergency, getting treatment for these diseases is not goi
easy.

Generally speaking, you have two options to treat water. Th
using chlorine bleach, as we mentioned earlier—you need
an emergency stock of bleach for these situations. The othe
is boiling the water to get rid of the impurities and contar
One thing to keep in mind, though, is that these two option
filter water, so you'll have to do that first before purificati
can filter the water if it looks murky by letting it sit still for
until the suspended particles can settle in the bottom of t
due to their weight. After that, use layers of cotton or paper
or even coffee filters to trap the sediments and filter the wate

Chapter 8: Non-Perishable and Long Shelf-Life Food Storage

While water is the most important thing for survival, food is also critical, and you need to take steps to ensure that your household won't starve in an emergency situation. Fortunately, food is much easier to store than water, and you get a lot more options too. Non-perishable foods with long shelf life can last up to years without spoiling, and they come in handy during emergencies and can keep you and your family full until things return to normal. Moderation is key here because you don't want to store too much food that will eventually rot.

Long-Term Food Storage

Long-term food storage means the supplies that you keep for any unforeseen disasters in the future that might keep you off the grid for months. They are mostly dried foods and goods that can provide you and your family with nutrition and the basic calorie intake that you need to survive in times of distress. These non-perishable foods are often low in moisture and oil, and they can on average be stored for 20 to 30 years if you store them properly. Foods that can survive this long usually take some time to prepare and are high in calories, which you'll need in an emergency situation. So, what should you get?

As we said, you need foods that are low in moisture (under 10%) as well as oils and fats because these can survive for long without the risk of mold or bacteria that can spoil the food. In general, grains like wheat, white rice, and rolled oats are a great place to start. Then you have legumes, including peas, lentils, and dry beans. There's also pasta like elbow macaroni and dried corn. You should also get dried potatoes, dried and frozen vegetables/fruits, and salt as well as sugar.

How Much Should You Store?

This is a question that you need to ask yourself because stocking up years' worth of food doesn't make sense and is just a waste. The best way to go about it is to take into account your family's needs for food that could last for a few months. The great thing about non-perishable foods with a long shelf life is that they will last, whether you eat them or not. So, before deciding on how much food to store, ask yourself how many people you will want to feed. What kind of an emergency will you prepare for? A person prepping in a warzone will need much more food compared to a person prepping in an area that has the occasional hurricane or blizzard. Finally, consider the space that you have. Storage conditions make a lot of difference in the shelf life of the foods, so you can't overstock them. It's also a good idea to take into account neighbors and other people around you that might need some food in case of emergencies. So, store food that can keep you and your family self-sufficient for three or four months, and then add a bit more food in case of unforeseen disasters.

How to Store Food for the Long Term

Storage is key if you want your food to last for as long as it is intended. There's no sense in letting food that can last for 10 years spoil in one because you stored it poorly. It would end up costing you a lot of money that could be otherwise saved. Factors like temperature and exposure to light might affect the shelf life of non-perishable food.

Glass jars are your best friend for packaging and storing dry foods long-term. They come in all shapes and sizes, so you can select sizes suitable for the volume of food you want to store. You can store seeds and dry goods in these jars in bulk, not to mention dried vegetables and fruits that would be otherwise difficult to store without glass jars. These jars are a great option because glass doesn't allow oxygen or water to seep inside and compromise the stored food. They are durable and reusable, so if you're rotating your food supplies, you can use the same jars for newly purchased goods.

One thing to remember is that glass jars don't protect the food from light, so don't keep them exposed to direct sunlight, or else the food might spoil. Glass jars are also fragile and can easily break, so you should never store them in an area prone to earthquakes. Pro tip: Mason jars are specifically designed for food storage, so keep them in mind.

Mylar bags are another great option for long-term food storage. They're made of multilayered food-grade plastic and aluminum, and the food doesn't react to the aluminum since there is a plastic lining separating them. Mylar bags protect the food against oxygen and moisture and even light. They can be easily washed and reused, so they last for quite some time.

Rotating the Food

When it comes to long-term food storage, rotation is a must. You can easily store non-perishables like powdered milk and wheat, but if you use one of those cans or containers, how long can the food survive after that? Generally speaking, a bucket or can of non-perishable food can last for up to one year after you open it, but that is only if you keep it in an airtight environment that is cool and moisture-free.

Opening the canned foods aside, is it a good idea to rotate? Yes, always. You could easily incorporate some of these non-perishable foods into your daily menu, even if no disaster is looming. It will give your family the nutrition that they need, and more importantly, it will help them get used to these foods. One of the main problems with canned foods used in times of crisis is that many people take some time getting used to them, and it turns into an unpleasant experience. You also get to consume fresh food, which is always better for your diet. Non-perishable foods stored for a long time don't lose their caloric value. However, the protein quality might decrease over time, which is why the fresher you consume them, the better.

Moreover, consuming your long-term foods and rotating them ensures that they won't go to waste. You can spend decades without going through a disaster, and then one day, chaos might ensue out of the blue. So, you should have fresh foods lying around, ready for use, instead of those cans you had stored in the 90s.

Chapter 9: Perishable Food Storage

As the name implies, perishable food has a significantly shorter lifespan compared to that with long shelf life. Storage is key with perishable foods because they will rot and spoil even before their short shelf life if incorrectly stored. When we talk about perishable food, we usually mean things that have to be consumed within the span of days or weeks, a few months at the most. This includes dairy, fruits, vegetables, eggs, meat, poultry, and seafood. When it comes to perishable foods, you need moderation because if it spoils, you can't eat it, so it will be wasted money. These are some things to keep in mind.

Use It First

In an emergency, you have to use the perishable food first. Canned goods and frozen vegetables/fruits have a long shelf life, so they can be consumed months later if the situation doesn't improve. Eggs, dairy, and meats, on the other hand, will quickly spoil.

Store It Properly

A lot of people just toss their perishable foods anywhere in the refrigerator, but this is a big mistake. There needs to be a certain order to how you arrange things in your fridge so you can preserve them for as long as possible. Foods that are ready to eat go on top, and keep the meat and poultry separately toward the bottom because they might contaminate other foods that you store. It's also a good idea to keep meats in bowls/trays because leaks might affect other products in your refrigerator. Fruit and vegetables are usually stored in the bottom bin. Spices, sauces, and other condiments go on the door shelves—the warmest part of the fridge.

Always keep the fridge clean, and don't throw things haphazardly inside. Instead, evenly arrange your produce so the air can flow easily. Keep the temperature between 32°F and 40°F. When it comes to storage, you need to be mindful of how you use the fridge. Keep the door to the freezer and refrigerator closed as much as possible to keep a steady temperature. Use a refrigerator thermostat to check the temperature and keep it steady.

Mind the Expiry Dates

For perishable foods, you have to track the storage times. No matter how properly you store these products, they have a certain expiry date, after which they become unusable or at the very least taste differently. They can also be unsafe to eat. So, when you store eggs, milk, meat, fruits, vegetables, or other perishable foods, remember when exactly you stored them and compare them to the expected shelf life for each. In an emergency, this will help you eat the foods that are closest to spoiling first and then work your way toward those that can last for a while longer.

Tips

Use Containers: With perishables, it's best that you keep the food in closed containers; it will extend the shelf life of the product.

When in Doubt, Throw Away: Unless the situation is extremely dire, when you doubt the quality of the perishable food, don't eat it. Never eat from cans that are swollen or dented or corroded, no matter how well the food looks. If the food smells or looks weird, don't eat it. Chances are, it's spoiled.

Avoid Room Temperature: While some fruits and vegetables are best kept at room temperature, most perishable foods need to be stored in refrigerators. If you have some food that was left at room temperature for over a few hours, get rid of it.

Regularly Clean the Fridge: As we mentioned earlier, keeping your refrigerator clean is essential to keep other foods from spoiling. Make it a part of your usual routine. Get rid of spoiled and rotten food as soon as possible. Keep an eye on foods that are about to expire so you can eat them first. These are small details that can make a world of difference, especially in an emergency where wasted food is a luxury that you cannot afford.

Eat the Opened Food: If you open a can of perishable food, thaw meat or poultry, or cook something, it should be eaten as soon as possible. Generally speaking, the most you should wait before eating the food in these cases is 3 or 4 days. After that, it is best that you get rid of the thawed meat if you haven't cooked it or that leftover lasagna from last week.

Cook it: Want to make your perishable food last longer? Cook it! With proper storage, your perishable food will last for a few more days than if you left it raw. Moreover, if you don't want to eat food that has been cooked for a few days, then you can share it with your neighbors. Check and see what food might spoil in your fridge, cook them, and invite your neighbors over for a nice meal or two. It definitely beats letting it spoil or eating five-day old lasagna.

Chapter 10: Cooking Off-the-Grid

Storing food is one thing. Cooking it in times of crisis is a whole other challenge. If a storm or hurricane affected the power lines or gas supply, you might be faced with the challenge of having to cook something without the usual luxury of a stove and oven. There's only so much canned food that you can eat before you get fed up with non-perishables. Moreover, if disaster strikes, you will most likely have a lot of perishable poultry, meat, and eggs in your fridge that you should cook before they go to waste.

Open-Fire Cooking

Primitive man made do with open-fire cooking, and so can you. If the weather outside your home permits it (for those living near woods or in open spaces), an open fire can be a great way to cook and is great for several reasons. For starters, you don't need a lot of fuel to get an open fire going. Sure, fuel might help, but you can still cook off the grid with no fuel. You will just need some tree logs and paper or other firewood to keep the fire going.

You can dig a hole in the ground and cook your meals—it actually results in delicious chicken and/or meat! The great thing about open-fire cooking is that you can even use a fireplace in your house. As long as there is a flame, you can cook. Just decide on how you'll do it: hanging the food over the fire, using a Dutch oven, spits, or other means at your disposal. Pro tip: create a fire pit or ring to cook instead of just making an open fire at any place, which might be dangerous and can lead to wildfires and other problems.

Gas, Charcoal, or Electric Grills

This is a cool way to cook your food, and a lot of people use either option without any emergencies. If your power lines are down, but the gas is working fine, you can cook using a gas grill, which doesn't need electricity to run. Gas grills add a special flavor to the food, so you'll end up having a nice meal after all. If, however, it was the other way around and you found yourself with electricity and no gas, you can use an electric grill if you have one. The food won't have that smoky flavor that you'd get from a gas one, but it is still very functional. Charcoal grills, on the other hand, require just charcoal, so you can use them if you have no power or gas.

Wood Stoves

Wood stoves are excellent for more than just cooking. They can heat your house in extreme cold, and they require no electricity to run, so they can be used if there is a blackout. Heating aside, wood stoves can be used for cooking and are quite practical. If you didn't know it already, different types of wood bring a unique flavor to the food, from sweet to smoky and oaky. You can get creative with the type of wood you use to cook.

Solar Stoves

Solar stoves don't require any electricity or gas to run, and they run on solar energy, making them an ideal option for people living in places where blackouts and/or gas pipeline disruptions are frequent. A solar oven works just like your regular one, though cooking the food might take a bit longer. Still, it is a convenient option that won't bother you with having to find fuel or going outside to make a fire. Some people who try to make the shift toward clean energy use this kind of stove instead of regular ones, considering how sustainable it is and how much better for the environment it can be.

Portable Stoves

Portable stove technology has greatly advanced over the past few years. There are plenty of options for you now that can help you cook fine meals without electricity or gas. Rocket stoves, for example, use little fuel and are a very efficient way to cook off-the-grid. They are compact and can be easily carried around anywhere you go. You have other options like camping stoves, which are also efficient and easily movable.

Tips for Cooking Off-the-Grid

Prepare in Advance: As this whole book is about prepping, you need to take into account your potential future needs. You will store food and water to keep your household running normally in an emergency, and fuel is also important. Depending on which cooking method you choose, you should stock up on the necessary fuel. So, if you're going to use a charcoal grill in blackouts, for example, then you need to have packs of charcoal stored safely so you can use them when you need to.

You should know what fuel is most easily found in the market. In the previous example, we mentioned charcoal as the fuel source. In some places, charcoal might not be in abundance. If you meet a problem like that, you should have a backup plan and find yourself another off-the-grid cooking option. **Don't Overstock:** As we've been saying since the beginning, moderation is key, so you don't risk wasting your money on products that will spoil. If you're storing charcoal, account for at least two hot meals per day for your family and stock up accordingly. Measure out the quantity that could keep you going for a few weeks or a month. Any more than that, and the charcoal or other types of fuel might go bad, especially if poorly stored.

Section 3: Non-Food Prepping

Chapter 11: First Aid!

It wouldn't be an overstatement to say that first-aid supplies are just as important as food and water. You're prepping for a serious situation or a natural catastrophe, and nothing you store will matter if you don't have the necessary tools to tend to injuries without having to wait for first responders. In times of crisis, it could take days or even weeks to reach damaged locations. What will you do then? You cannot wait for that to happen. Instead, pack everything you might need to tend to potential injuries, and then some.

Medication

Before we can even talk about the essentials of a first-aid kit, you have to stock up on necessary medication. If you or any of your family members have a certain prescription that you need regularly, then this is your first priority—examples include heart or asthma medication. Make sure you have a few weeks' supplies of essential medicine like that because it can save your life if you can't reach a pharmacy or have medicine delivered to you.

Prescription medication aside, you should also have an emergency stock of generic medicine like painkillers, antacids, laxatives, anti-diarrhea meds, and others that you could possibly need if you are stranded from the outside world.

First Aid Supplies

You shouldn't just buy your average kit from the pharmacy. When it comes to prepping for a disaster, the more first aid supplies you have, the better. You need:

- Multiple cleansing wipes (sting-free)
- Antibiotic ointment packs,

- Hydrocortisone creams,
- Trauma pads,
- Chewable aspirin tablets,
- Gauze dressing pads of different sizes,
- Conforming gauze rolls,
- Instant cold compresses,
- Emergency blankets,
- First aid tape roll,
- Sling bandages,
- Adhesive plastic bandages in abundance (also different sizes),
- Knuckle fabric bandages,
- Thermometers (more than one),
- Plastic tweezers,
- Scissors, gloves, and fingertip fabric bandages,
- Face shields/masks,
- Hot pads,
- Zip stitch bandages
- Any other tools that you might need to deal with an injury.

First aid supplies can be stored for a long time (3 to 5 years on average), and they will always prove useful. This is one of the few areas where it's fine if you get more than your needs. Extra antibiotics might save your neighbor's life or help others in need.

Additional Items

Emergency kits aside, you should consider some of the smaller health items like prescription eyeglasses, contact lens solutions, eye drops, infant formula for newborns, and other things that will prove invaluable in case you can't go to the pharmacy or your doctor. Also, stock up on hand sanitizers and face masks because they can protect you from potential infections.

Storage

Like anything we mentioned so far, storing your first aid kid properly is important. It needs to be put in a cool and dry place, away from moisture and direct sunlight. Keep an eye on your kit and regularly check it to see if any items have expired. This isn't like food where you can consume the perishables before they go bad. If an antibiotic or cream is about to expire, get rid of it and get a new one. Moreover, regularly update your kit with any essential needs that might arise. For instance, the first-aid kit before COVID-19 is much different than after, so you need to take public health concerns into account.

When you store the first aid kit in a place, make sure you don't move it around. It needs to be at an easily accessible location around your house so you wouldn't waste time looking for it. Some people even recommend having a spare emergency kit in your car in case something happened while you were on the road.

Chapter 12: Sanitary Essentials

Sometimes, in an extreme emergency, sanitation and hygiene can be the difference between surviving and dying. These aren't items you use for luxury, but they are sanitary essentials that you use to stave off infections and other illnesses. Reading this, you might be thinking of toilet paper and your deodorant, but there are many things that you will miss if you find yourself stranded and unable to get your basic needs.

Sanitation

Keeping yourself and the area clean is crucial during disasters, as we said. The first and foremost item you need to have plenty of is toilet paper. You shouldn't hoard and stock more than your family's needs for a duration of a few weeks or months, but as many people have learned in the pandemic, toilet paper is an essential item that easily runs out when people panic buy. You won't wait for the disaster to happen. Always have an emergency stock of toilet paper that your family can use. You'll also want to have some toilet cleaners and sterilizing solutions so you can keep your toilets clean until the situation improves. Toilets are breeding grounds for bacteria, and leaving them unclean is a disaster waiting to happen. Moreover, if you don't have running water, you should find a location for your sanitation needs that is away from any water source, or else you'll risk contaminating it.

Hand Washing, Bathing, and Oral Health

As we said, keeping clean in times of disaster is not a luxury. You don't have to shower twice a day, but you need to keep clean so that your wounds can heal properly and remain uninfected. Add an emergency stock of soaps so you can wash your hands as often as you can—which is crucial before cooking or handling food and water in general. You don't need to have a hundred soap bars, but just enough to keep you going. Calculate, on average, how much soap and detergents your family uses per week, and store a few weeks or months' worth.

You should also have some shampoo stored. It might not be essential, but it can make things more comfortable during a distressing time. It can also help you avoid scalp or skin conditions that might arise if you don't shower often. The same goes for your oral health. You should have some toothpaste stored for emergencies so you can regularly brush your teeth, especially if you or any of your family have sensitive teeth. Store an additional toothbrush for each of your family members. They can even be used for scrubbing and cleaning, so they're always useful to have around.

Feminine Products

Having a stock of feminine products is a must so that every woman in the household can have her needs covered in a crisis. From tampons and pads to menstrual cups, it's crucial that part of your prepping covers any feminine products in abundance because these are essentials that a woman cannot live without.

Miscellaneous

There are other items that you can store, just in case. Deodorants, hair conditioners, combs, brushes, and other items that might not be necessary for survival often prove to be life-savers (in the metaphorical sense) and help make the best out of an uncomfortable situation. Air fresheners also help and can help make your place smell nice, especially if the weather is bad outside and you cannot exactly open the windows.

Chapter 13: Essential Emergency Items

Last but not least, there are some essential items that you need to have during an emergency. Food and water aren't everything. There are some smaller items that will help you survive and get through the ordeal, and without them, things will be much more difficult.

Light: You need to have several flashlights stored so you could find your way around the house in a blackout. Candles also help, which is why you will need to store some matches as well (it's best to buy waterproof matches). Keep a decent supply of spare batteries for the flashlights and any other electronics. Solar-powered flashlights are a good tool to have and will prove useful in a long-term emergency.

Safety: We dedicated an entire chapter to cooking off-the-grid, which might be a bit risky. Needless to say, in a blizzard or hurricane, no fire trucks will be around. So, you should have fire extinguishers filled and ready to use at any time. They can save your life one day.

Map and Compass: Technology is great and everything, but it's too unreliable and can easily fail you. With a good old-fashioned map and compass, you can never go wrong, and they'll help you navigate your way out of the area if you ever need to do that.

Multi-Purpose Knife: A multi-purpose steel army knife doesn't just look cool. It can serve a lot of functions, and more often than not, it proves quite useful in emergencies.

Various Items: An emergency whistle can help rescuers find you if you're too out of sight. So can flares, which offer visibility in dark places. You should always have plenty of duct tape stored because it proves very useful in tight spots and can help stop a leak or fix something that you urgently need.

Conclusion

Preparing for the Worst so You Can Live Your Best

I would hope that by this point if you've read the book and didn't just skip to the conclusion after reading the introduction, you're beginning to think that it isn't such a bad idea to do a little prepping.

However, if you still need a little nudge, let me ask you a question. Do you have homeowners insurance? Auto Insurance? How about life insurance? These are all things we buy, hoping we never need them. Prepping, if done in moderation, is the same thing, for the most part. The things you purchase for prepping are actually things that not only can be used but also should be used. Rotating your supplies, as we've explained earlier, is important and will always provide you with fresh and clean water and food.

Regardless of whether or not you've decided to begin taking steps to be a prepper, in moderation, I think we can all learn some lessons from 2020.

COVID has taught us that we always need to keep a couple of extra packs (Costco cases) of TP on hand. We need to make sure we have a couple of weeks' worth of food on hand just in case there are shortages. And maybe it's time to get that wine cellar you've always been dreaming about because you never know when your Governor will stop alcohol sales during a state of emergency.

If you want to know more about the effective use of alcohol during an emergency, read my upcoming book series: Brewing for Fun and Survival.

There are also lessons to be found in the winter storm that hit Texas. The winter storm that blanketed at least 25 counties in Texas left millions without power for days. Without power, people's homes were destroyed as pipes froze and burst. Winter storms are so rare in Texas they are probably never part of the municipal planning meetings, and as a result, the state had no plan in place for how to de-ice the roads. This resulted in people who were suddenly without water not being able to leave their house to go out looking for life essentials. Of course, honestly, most Texans have no idea how to drive in winter weather anyway.

Sure, we could say that this was a once-in-a-lifetime event and is unlikely to happen for another hundred years, but many of the counties that were affected by the storm are counties that are also vulnerable to hurricanes, which are far more likely to occur. So, while the winter storm was something that a reasonable person wouldn't think to prepare for, the same preparation done for a potential hurricane could have been helpful during the winter storm.

While you're thinking about what preparation with moderation means to you, pick up that extra pack of TP the next time you're at Costco. Buy an extra pack of Lysol wipes just in case. Pick up an extra bag of rice because you never know when it may be useful, or the shelves may suddenly be empty.

And once you've started prepping, check out my book series "Brewing for Fun and Survival." Learning how to make beer, wine, and mead is not only fun and a great defense against the government banning alcohol sales; it leaves you with a product you can use to barter for the things you can't produce yourself.

References

BBC News. (2021, June 3). JBS: FBI says Russia-linked group hacked meat supplier. BBC. Retrieved from https://www.bbc.com/news/world-us-canada-57338896

Best emergency water storage containers for your home. (2017, August 25). Retrieved from Theprepared.com website: https://theprepared.com/homestead/reviews/best-two-week-emergency-water-storage-containers/

Bloomberg. (n.d.). Bloomberg News. Retrieved from https://www.bloomberg.com/news/articles/2021-06-04/hackers-breached-colonial-pipeline-using-compromised-password

Brooks, A. (2017, February 16). Food safety - safe storage for perishable foods. Retrieved from Ext.vt.edu website: https://blogs.ext.vt.edu/eatsmart-movemore/2017/02/16/safe-storage-perishable-foods/

Build A Kit. (n.d.). Retrieved from Ready.gov website: https://www.ready.gov/kit

Chrobak, U. (2020, August 17). The US has more power outages than any other developed country.Here's why. Retrieved from Popsci.com website: https://www.popsci.com/story/environment/why-us-lose-power-storms/

Clever Prototypes, L. L. C. (n.d.). Causes of Natural Disaster. Retrieved from Storyboardthat.com website: https://www.storyboardthat.com/lesson-plans/natural-disasters

Deluxe Family First Aid Kit. (n.d.). Retrieved from Redcross.org website: https://www.redcross.org/store/deluxe-family-first-aid-kit/321275.html?utm_source=RCO&utm_medium=Referral&utm_term=Deluxe_family_first_aid_kit&utm_campaign=Survival_Kit_Supplies

Food. (n.d.). Retrieved from Ready.gov website: https://www.ready.gov/food

Food sustainability and geopolitics. (2017, March 24). Retrieved from Eiu.com website: https://foodsustainability.eiu.com/food-sustainability-and-geopolitics/

Goldschmitt, D. (2009). Types of Disasters. In Medical Disaster Response (pp. 123–143). CRC Press.

Homeowners: Respond to natural gas disruptions. (n.d.). Retrieved from Energy.gov website: https://www.energy.gov/ceser/emergency-preparedness/community-guidelines-energy-emergencies/homeowners-respond-natural-gas

How much food should I store for an emergency? (n.d.). Retrieved from Readywise.com website: https://readywise.com/blogs/readywise-blog/how-much-food-should-i-store-for-an-emergency

Kylene. (2020a, June 16). How to package dry foods in Mylar bags for long-term storage. Retrieved from Theprovidentprepper.org website: https://theprovidentprepper.org/how-to-package-dry-foods-in-mylar-bags-for-long-term-storage/

Kylene. (2020b, July 18). Packaging dry foods in glass jars for long-term food storage. Retrieved from Theprovidentprepper.org website: https://theprovidentprepper.org/packaging-dry-foods-in-glass-jars-for-long-term-food-storage/

Levitt, T., Blight, G., van der Zee, B., Hilaire, E., & McDonald, J. (2020, September 15). Covid and farm animals: nine pandemics that changed the world. The Guardian. Retrieved from http://www.theguardian.com/environment/ng-interactive/2020/sep/15/covid-farm-animals-and-pandemics-diseases-that-changed-the-world

McKenna, A. (2020, September 10). How to prepare for a long-term power outage. Retrieved from Constellation.com website: https://blog.constellation.com/2020/09/10/how-to-prepare-for-a-long-term-power-outage/

Methods to transport emergency water from source to home. (2016, August 17). Retrieved from Modernsurvivalblog.com website: https://modernsurvivalblog.com/preps/methods-to-transport-emergency-water-from-source-to-home/

Mott, A. (2020, March 24). Sanitation and hygiene during an emergency. Retrieved from Beprepared.com website:

https://beprepared.com/blogs/articles/sanitation-and-hygiene-during-an-emergency-2

Poindexter, J. (2016, November 29). Survival cooking: 18 off-grid cooking methods without electricity. Retrieved from Morningchores.com website: https://morningchores.com/survival-cooking/

Prepared Mom Team. (2014, June 9). 5+ Ways to Cook Off-grid without power. Retrieved from Momwithaprep.com website: https://momwithaprep.com/5-ways-cook-grid/

Rea, F. (2021, February 18). 15 items everyone should have in their at-home emergency kit. Business Insider. Retrieved from https://www.businessinsider.com/home-emergency-kit-products

Rotating Long-Term Food Storage. (n.d.). Retrieved from Familysurvivalplanning.com website: https://www.familysurvivalplanning.com/rotating-long-term-foods.html

Survival Kit Supplies. (n.d.). Retrieved from Redcross.org website: https://www.redcross.org/get-help/how-to-prepare-for-emergencies/survival-kit-supplies.html

Understand Produce Contamination. (2017, May 2). Retrieved from Aiche.org website: https://www.aiche.org/resources/publications/cep/2017/may/understand-produce-contamination

Water Main Breaks. (n.d.). Retrieved from Bedfordma.gov website: https://www.bedfordma.gov/department-of-public-works/webforms/water-main-breaks

Why power outages occur. (n.d.). Retrieved from Wisconsinpublicservice.com website: https://www.wisconsinpublicservice.com/services/power-occur

(N.d.-a). Retrieved from Nap.edu website: https://www.nap.edu/read/6425/chapter/8

(N.d.-b). Retrieved from Statesman.com website: https://www.statesman.com/story/news/politics/politifact/2021/03/05/texas-natural-gas-pipelines-dont-freeze-blame-power-outage/4596289001/

(N.d.-c). Retrieved from Wisc.edu website: https://foodsafety.wisc.edu/assets/pdf_Files/Emergency_water.pdf